Going Green

Contents

Hello fellow aliens!
What do you want to know
about planet Earth?

Going Green

Calling all aliens!

Are you planning a holiday to planet Earth?

Finn and Zeek are here to help.

'Going Green'
Published by MAVERICK ARTS PUBLISHING LTD

Studio 11, City Business Centre, 6 Brighton Road,

Horsham, West Sussex, RH13 5BB, +44 (0)1403 256941

© Maverick Arts Publishing Limited August 2019

A CIP catalogue record for this book is available at the British Library.

ISBN 978-1-84886-475-7

Maverick
publishing
www.maverickbooks.co.uk

Credits:

Finn & Zeek illustrations by Jake McDonald, Bright Illustration Agency
Cover: Jake McDonald/ Bright, Henry Georgi/ Robert Harding
Inside: Robert Harding: Lucas Vallecillos (6), Bernard Jaubert (8), Jochen Tach (9), Mike Kemp (11 & 12), Michael Interisano (13), Ken Welsh (14 & 15), Helmut Meyer zur Capellen (15), Steve Morgan (18), Dave Fleetham (18 & 19), Ashley Cooper (20), Tim Graham (21), Shutterstock: Beauty Studios (24), Robert Harding: W Eryk Jaegermann (25), Ethel Davis (25), Chris Hepburn (27)

White

This book is rated as: White Band (Guided Reading)

INCOMING MESSAGE

Dear Finn and Zeek,

We want to visit Earth, but our spaceship is powered by green energy!

Please can you show us how we can recharge it on Earth so that we can be prepared?

From Pick and Pock
(Planet Eco)

Humans use lots of power everyday. They use electricity to power their homes and technology, and fuel to power their transport. Electricity and fuel can be made in lots of different ways but not all of them are good for planet Earth.

Let's find out how humans are finding better ways to make electricity.

For years, humans have mainly made electricity using **non-renewable** materials. Non-renewable materials are things that humans take from the earth. They took millions of years to form. Once they are burned to **generate** electricity, these non-renewable materials are gone for good. There is no way for humans to get more, once they have used up these materials.

Coal

Examples of non-renewable energy are coal, natural gas and oil.

These non-renewable energy sources are also bad for the environment. Burning them creates **pollution** and harmful waste. Because of these reasons, humans are always trying to find new, cleaner ways to make electricity.

Renewable sources are the solution to this problem. When an energy source is renewable, it means that it can't be used up because it is a naturally occurring thing, like wind or sunlight.

These sources cause little to no harmful waste, which is why they are also called **green power**.

Green power sounds great! Why don't humans use it all the time?

The only problem is that humans can't control or store wind or sunlight. If the wind doesn't blow or the sun doesn't shine, sometimes there won't be enough power for everyone.

Let's find out more about green energy!

Super Skies   Wind Power

Wind power has been around for a very long time. Farmers have been using windmills to grind their crops and power machines for centuries.

Nowadays, humans use wind turbines to generate electricity. In order to create enough electricity to power lots of homes, they put lots of wind turbines together in wind farms.

To get as much wind as possible, wind farms have to be on flat, open areas where the wind blows at least 14 miles per hour. Some wind farms are out at sea, where the wind is strong.

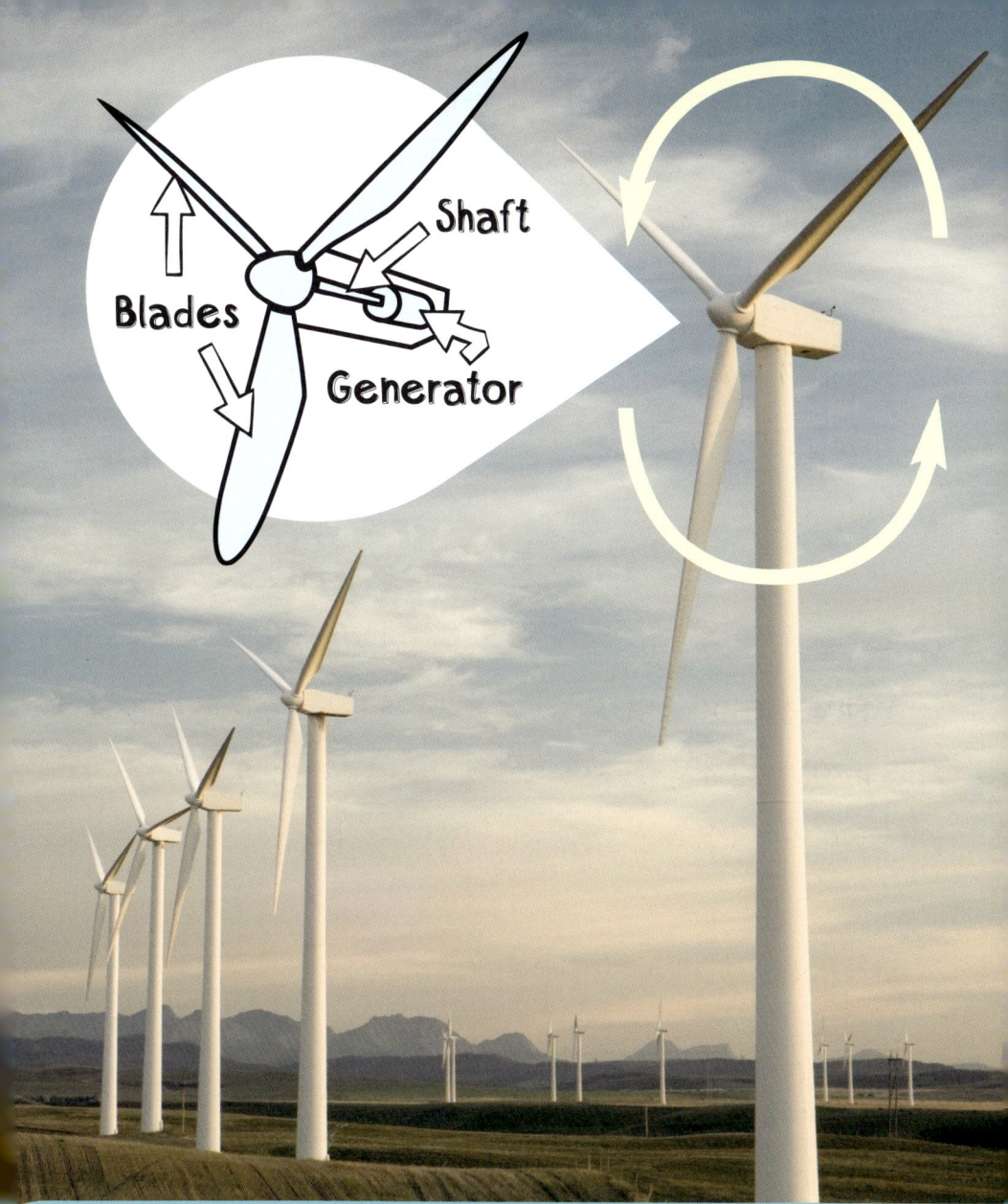

Blades

Shaft

Generator

Wind turns the blades, which spins the shaft, which connects to a generator. The spinning movement is what generates electricity.

'Solar' comes from the Latin word 'sol' which means 'sun'. So solar power is power that comes from the sun!

Solar power can be used in two different ways: as a heat source or to generate energy. People use solar panels on the roofs of their houses to produce hot water and to heat their homes.

Like wind turbines, lots of

To generate electricity, solar panels need something called **silicon,** which can be found in rocks, clay, soil and sand. In 1954, scientists discovered that silicon created an electric charge when lots of sunshine shone on it. With silicon in solar panels, the natural reaction can be used to create electricity.

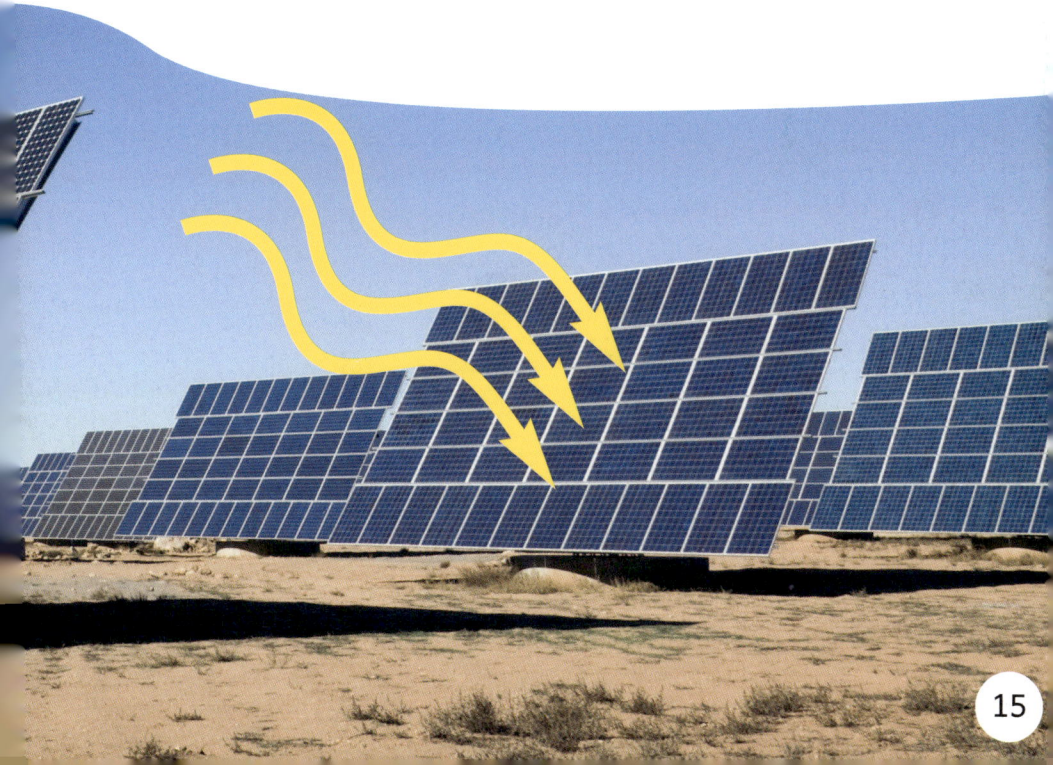

Dam

Reservoir

Intake

An intake controls the water flow.

'Hydro' comes from the Greek word for water so hydroelectric power is the way water can be used to create electricity. Electricity is generated by water the same way it is by wind: using turbines. Water turns the underwater turbines which are connected to generators.

Dams are used to create the right conditions for hydroelectric power to work. Dams are placed on big rivers where the flow of water will be strong and constant. Dams are a way to control the speed of the water's movement through the turbines. This creates a steady suppy of electricity.

Generator

Turbine

Power lines

River

Tidal turbines

Another way to use water for electricity is through tidal power. Using the movement of the sea, electricity can be generated through turbines.

Tidal power could be the most **efficient** out of all the green power sources.

This type of renewable energy is still quite new so scientists are still figuring out the best way to do this. However tidal power could become very useful because, unlike wind, tides are very predictable.

Biomass is a group of natural materials like wood and plants. These materials can then be burned to create heat, which in turn can be used to generate electricity.

Biomass can also create **biofuel** by letting it decompose or **ferment.** Biofuels can be used instead of petrol to power cars.

Rape seed is a plant that can be used to create biofuel.

Biomass comes from plants, so as long as humans are careful, they can keep growing new plants and they won't run out! If they aren't careful, biomass can lead to **deforestation**.

The clever thing about biomass is that certain types of rubbish are also considered to be biomass and can be burned as fuel. This means humans can turn the rubbish into power, as well as getting rid of it.

Geothermal Power

'Geo' means 'from the earth' and 'thermal' means 'heat', so geothermal means 'heat from the earth'. The centre of the Earth is very hot, so there is always a lot of heat coming from underground. Geothermal power is a good, clean way to heat houses.

Using pipes, a system pumps water into the earth to absorb the natural heat before taking it back above ground. A device called a heat pump then takes the heat and uses it to heat the air in a house.

Heat pump

This can also be done in reverse. On hot days, the system can take the heat from the air and put it back into the ground, to naturally cool the house.

Unusual Energy

Every day scientists are trying to find new, even cleaner ways to create green power. Sometimes these can be quite wacky!

Cow Poo (Methane)

Because of what they eat, cows create a lot of **methane**, either from when they fart or poo. Methane is a big contributor to **global warming** so one way scientists are trying to reduce the amount going into the atmosphere is to use it to create energy. The methane in cow poo can be used to create renewable electricity, vehicle fuel and renewable natural gas.

Algae

You know the slimy green stuff you find in ponds? It can produce oil. In fact, almost half of its body weight is oil. If extracted, this can become biofuel which we know is a more clean and efficient fuel than petrol.

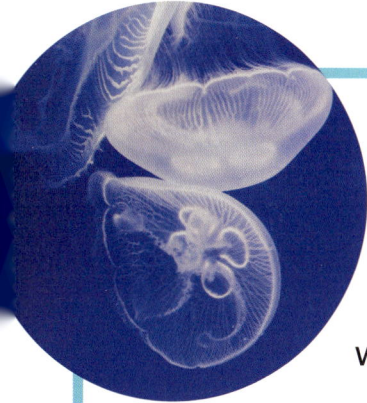

Jellyfish

Did you know that some kinds of jellyfish glow in the dark? Well, what makes them glow is a kind of goo which could also help generate solar power! Scientists are looking into how they can use this goo on solar panels to make them cheaper and even less harmful to create.

MESSAGE SENT

Dear Pick and Pock,

As you can see, humans have lots of green energy sources for your spaceship. While they are still not using 100% green energy, humans are increasing the amount of green energy they use everyday.

If you visit Earth, be sure to check out Iceland. Almost all of their electricity comes from green sources!

From,
Finn and Zeek x

Iceland's capital city, Reykjavík

1. Which of the below is **not** a green energy source?
a) Wind power
b) Coal
c) Biomass

2. Why are some energy sources 'renewable'?
a) Because they cannot be used up
b) Because they take a long time to form
c) Because they cause pollution

3. What is this part of a turbine called?

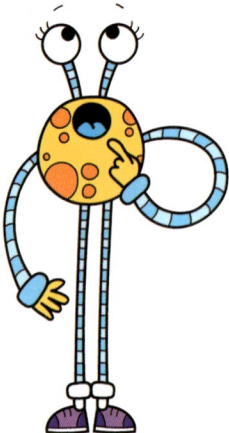

4. What is a group of solar panels called?

a) A party

b) A pack

c) A farm

5. What do wind and hydroelectric power have in common?

a) They are both non-renewable

b) They both use plants

c) They both use turbines

6. How can geothermal power be used?

a) To heat homes

b) To control water

c) To create solar panels

Turn over for answers

Index/Glossary

Green power pg 10, 19, 24
Renewable energy sources that cause little to no waste.

Methane pg 24
Methane is a gas and contributes to global warming.

Non-renewable pg 8-9
A power source that is used up completely to create electricity and takes a long time to form.

Pollution pg 9
When the environment is harmed by waste or chemicals.

Renewable pg 10-11, 19, 24
A power source that doesn't run out.

Silicon pg 15
An element that is found in rocks, clay, soil and sand that creates an electric charge in the sun.

Book Bands for Guided Reading

The Institute of Education book banding system is a scale of colours that reflects the various levels of reading difficulty. The bands are assigned by taking into account the content, the language style, the layout and phonics. Word, phrase and sentence level work is also taken into consideration.

Maverick Early Readers are a bright, attractive range of books covering the pink to white bands. All of these books have been book banded for guided reading to the industry standard and edited by a leading educational consultant.

Fiction

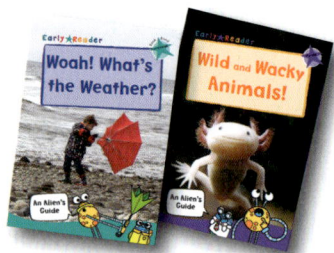

Non-fiction

To view the whole Maverick Readers scheme, visit our website at www.maverickearlyreaders.com

Or scan the QR code above to view our scheme instantly!